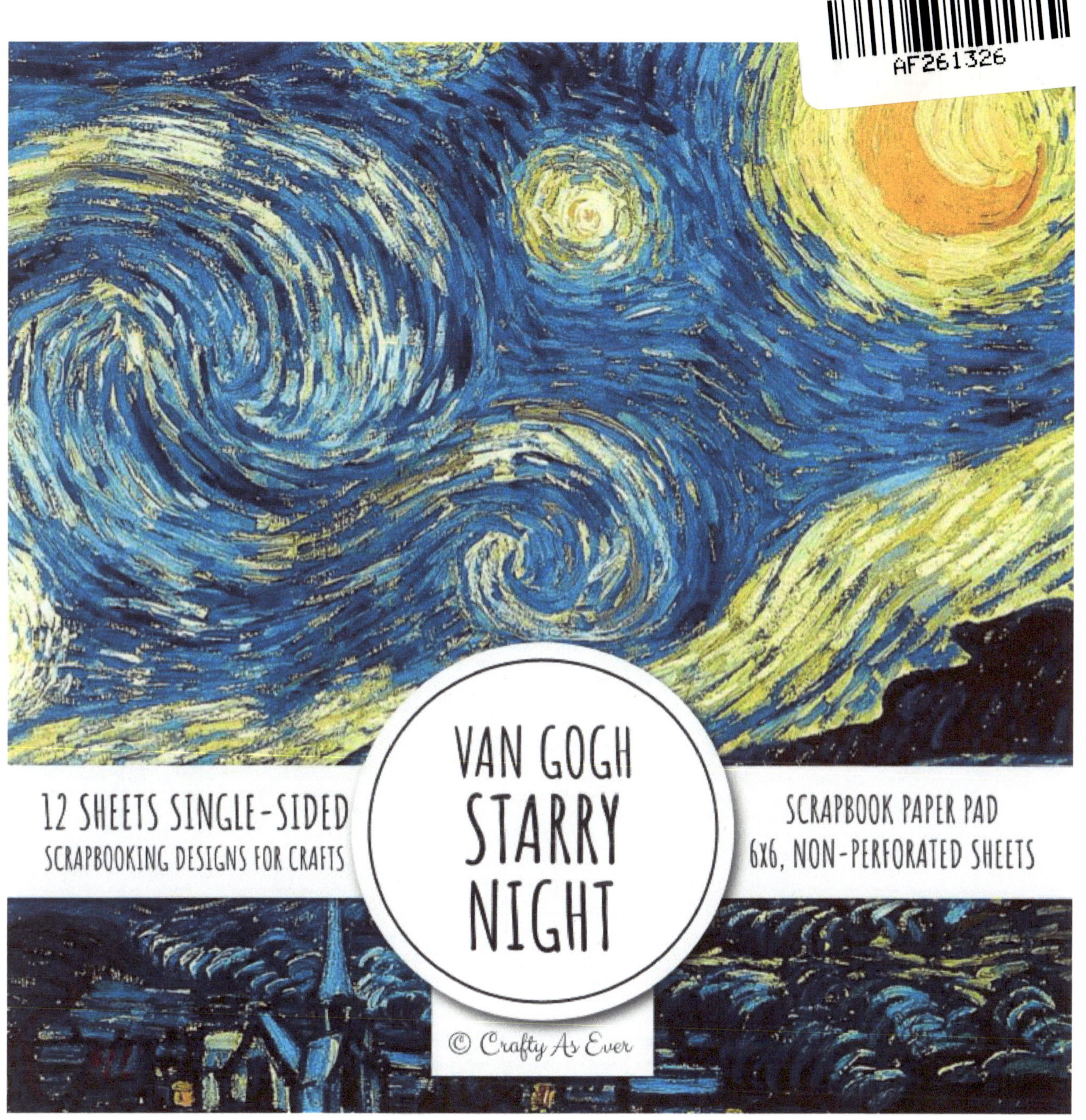
AF261326
VAN GOGH
STARRY
NIGHT
12 SHEETS SINGLE-SIDED
SCRAPBOOKING DESIGNS FOR CRAFTS
SCRAPBOOK PAPER PAD
6x6, NON-PERFORATED SHEETS
© Crafty As Ever

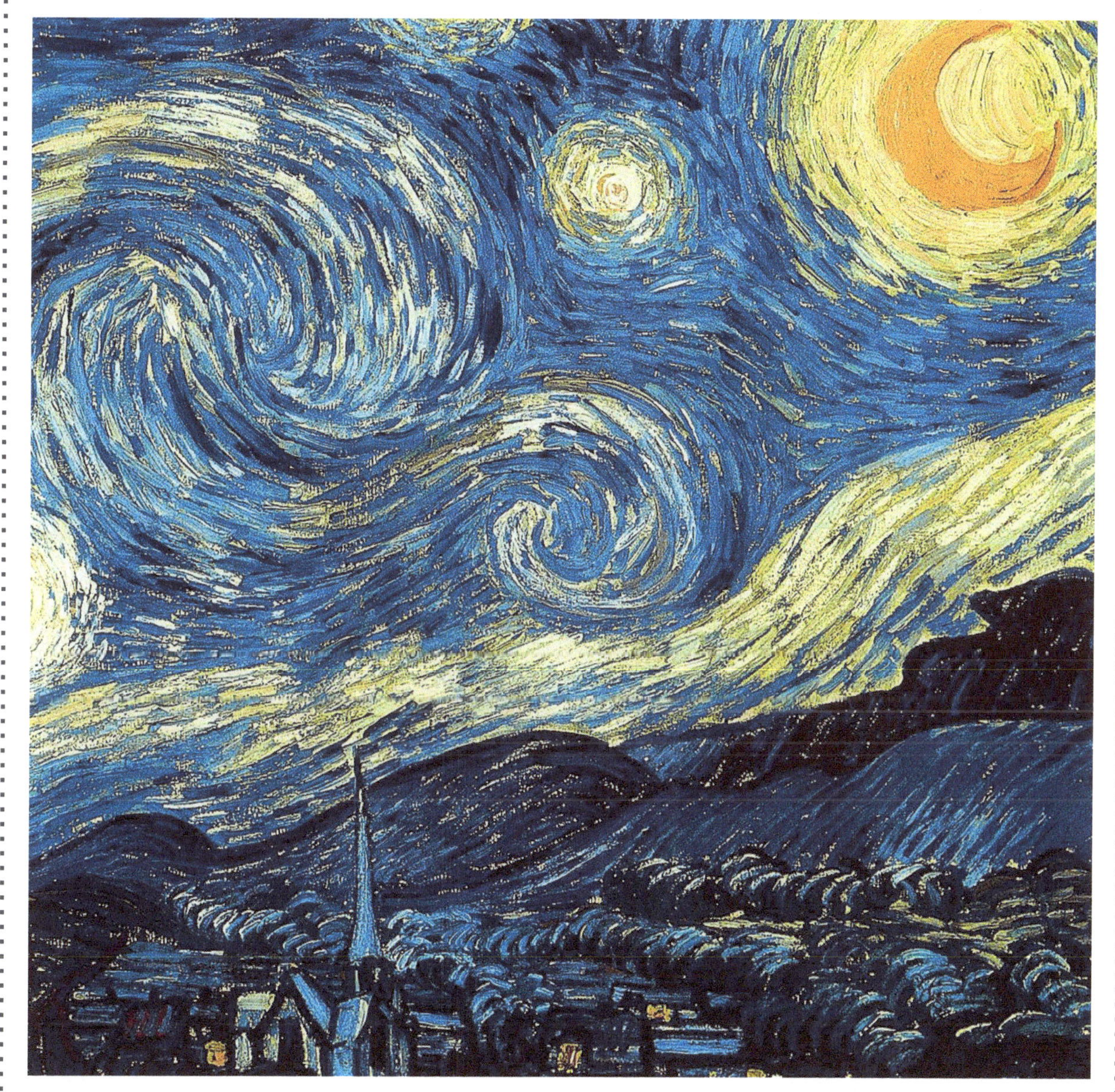

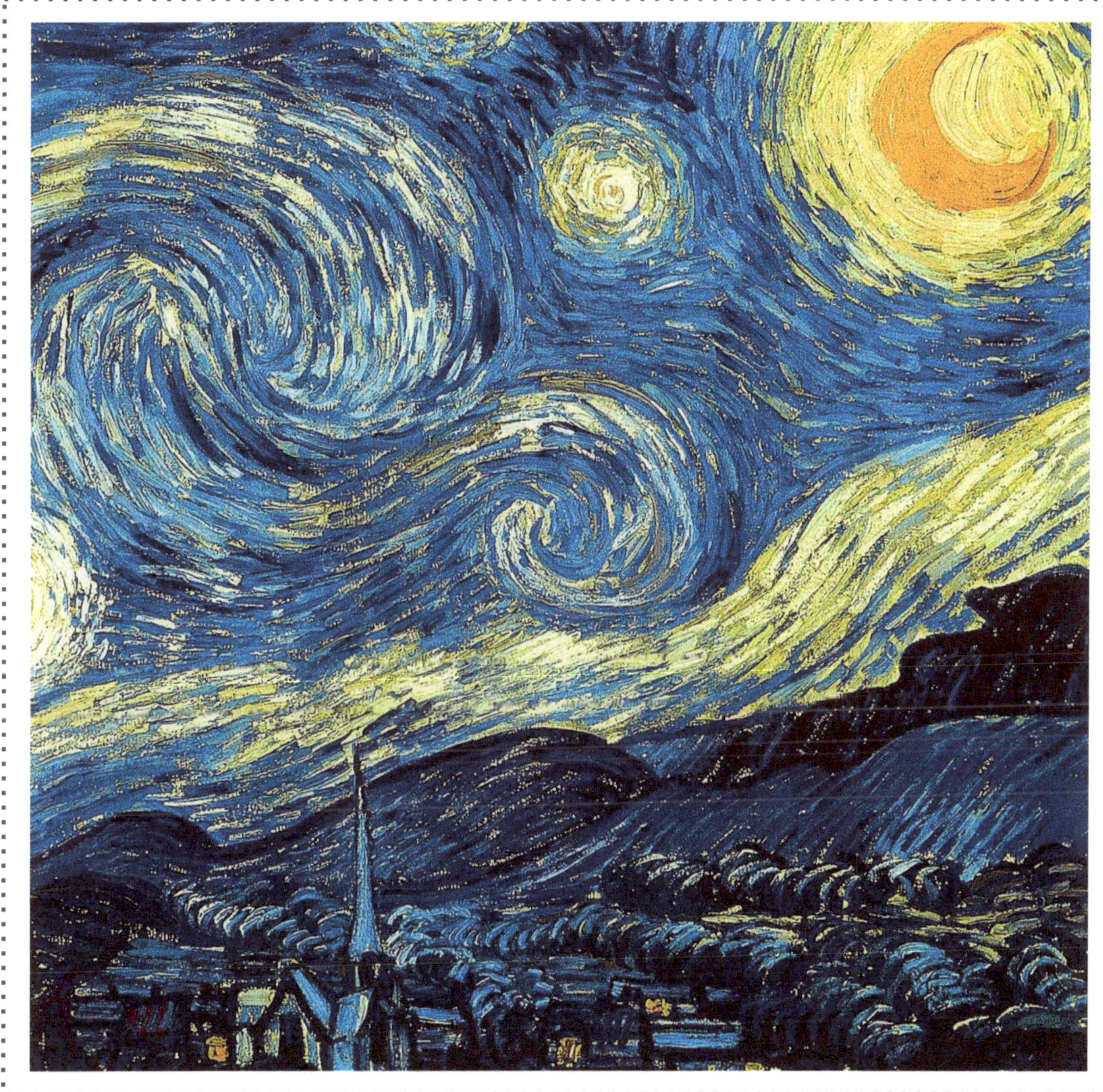

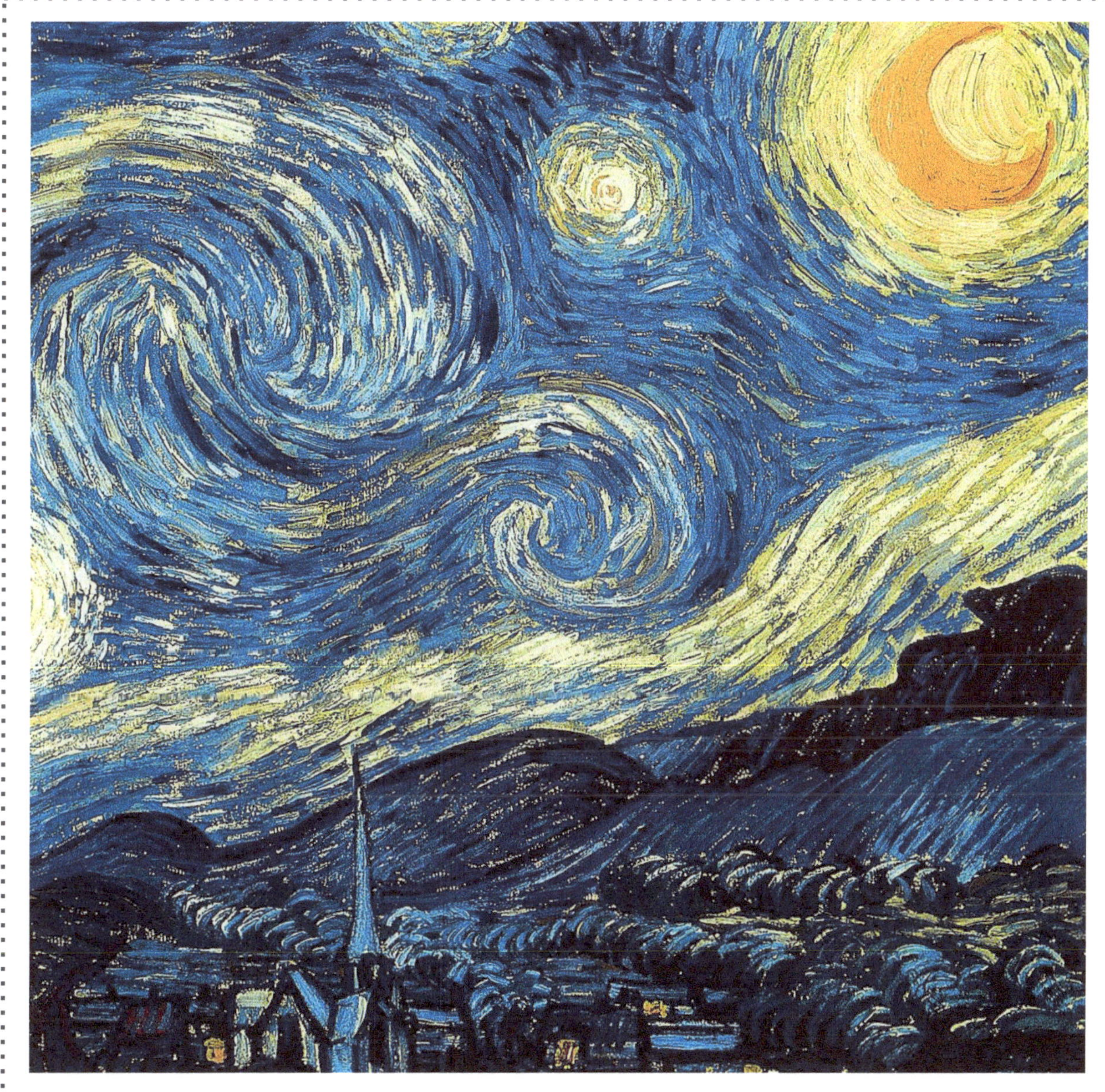

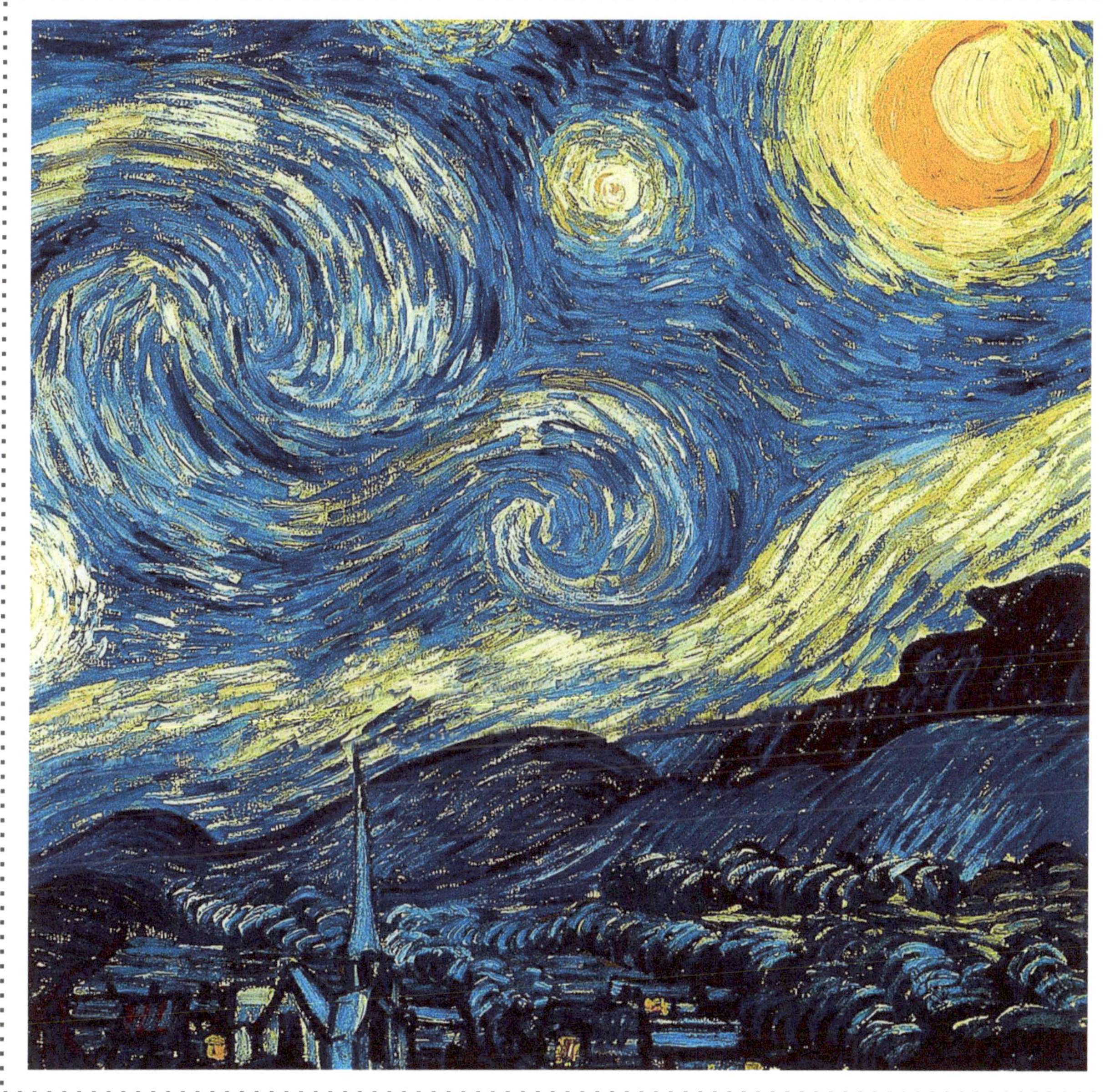

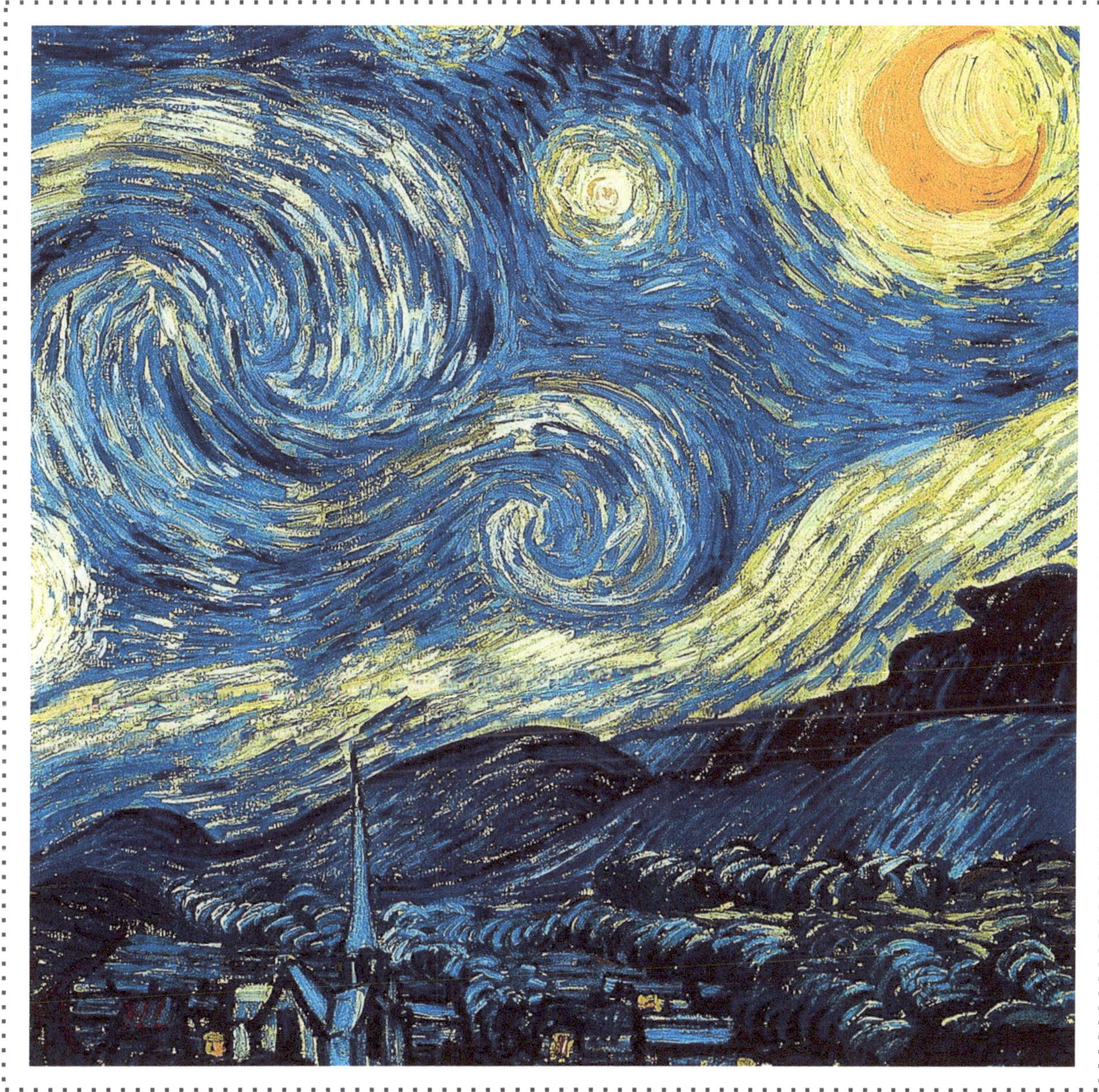

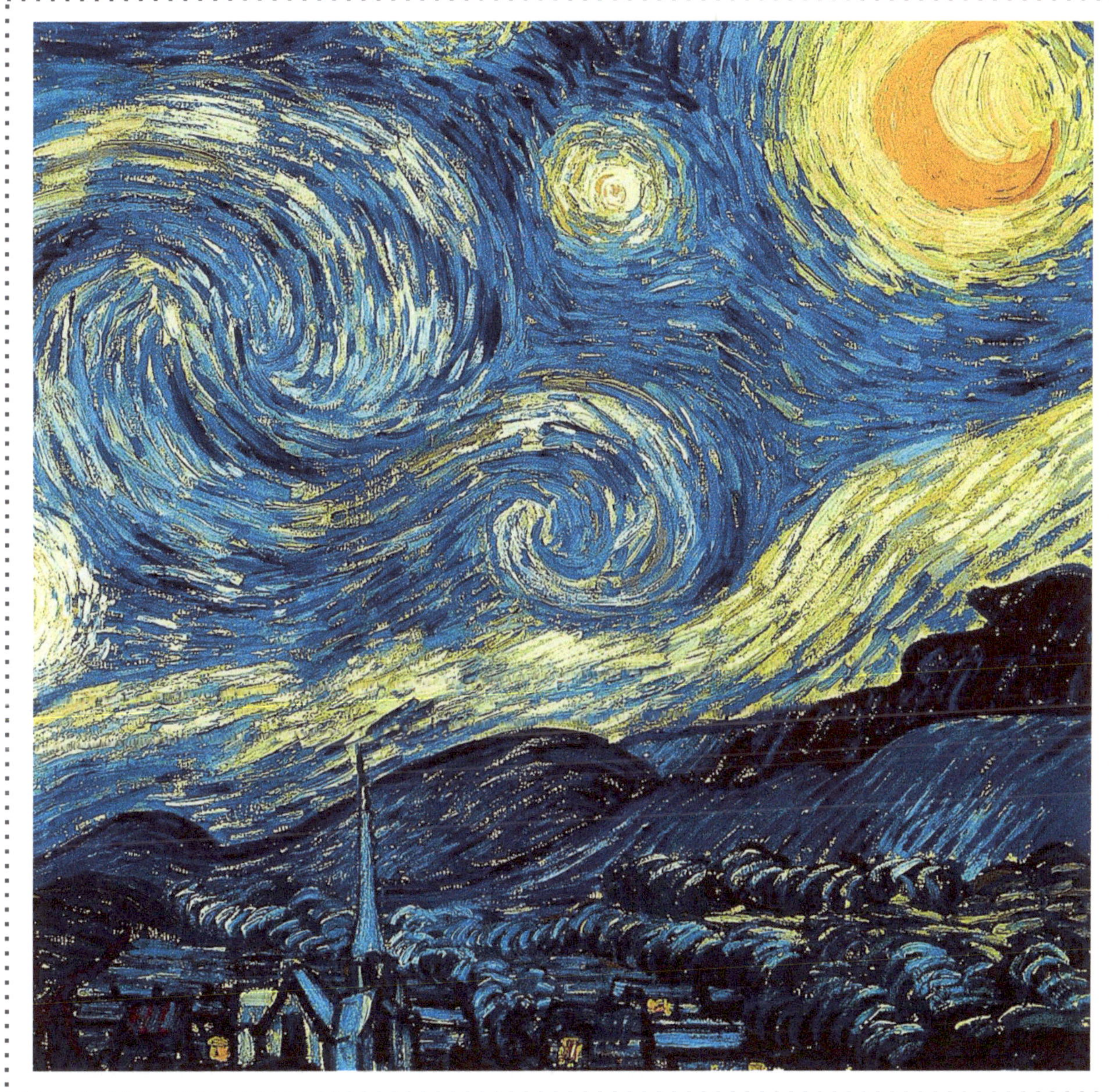

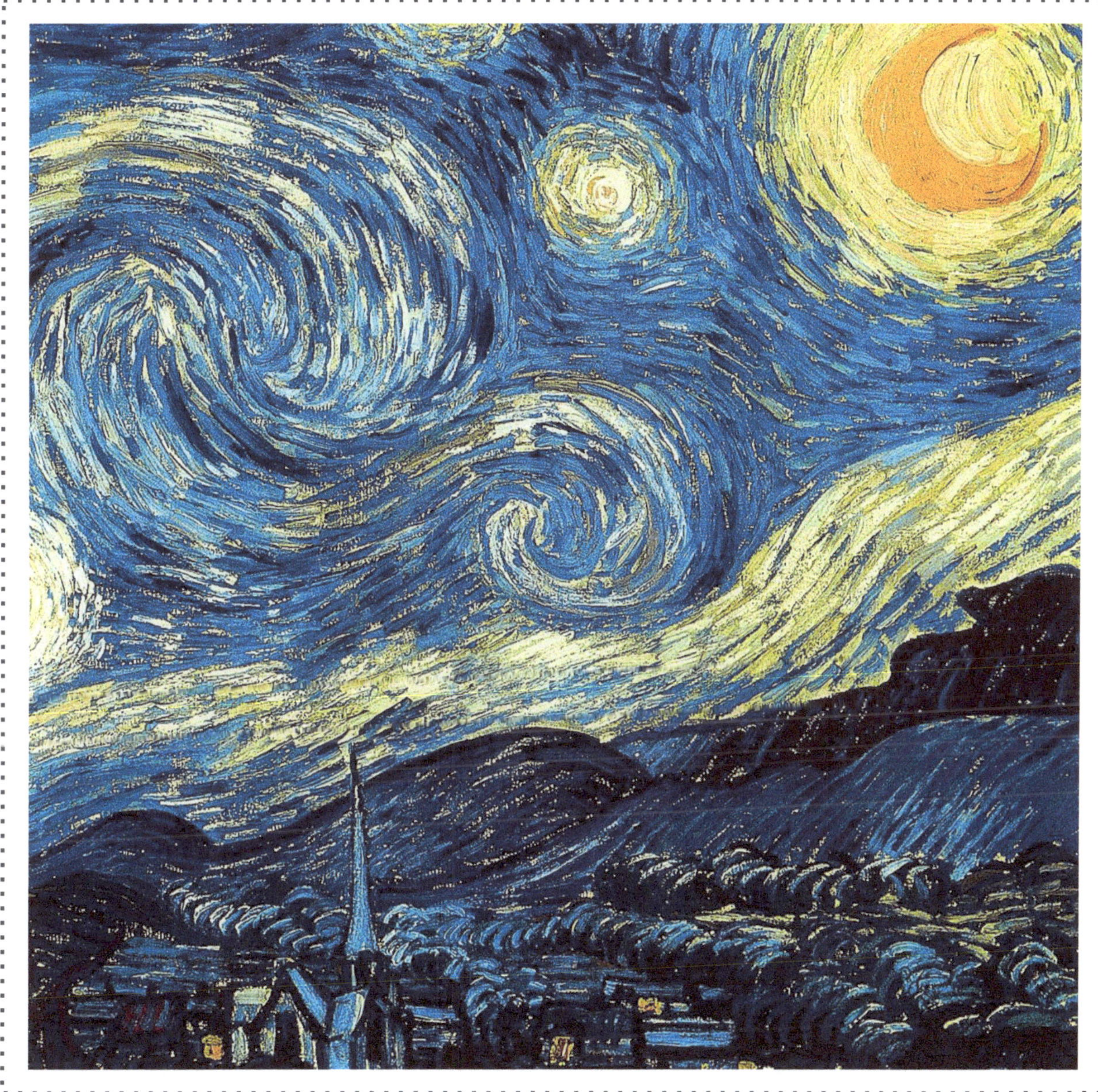

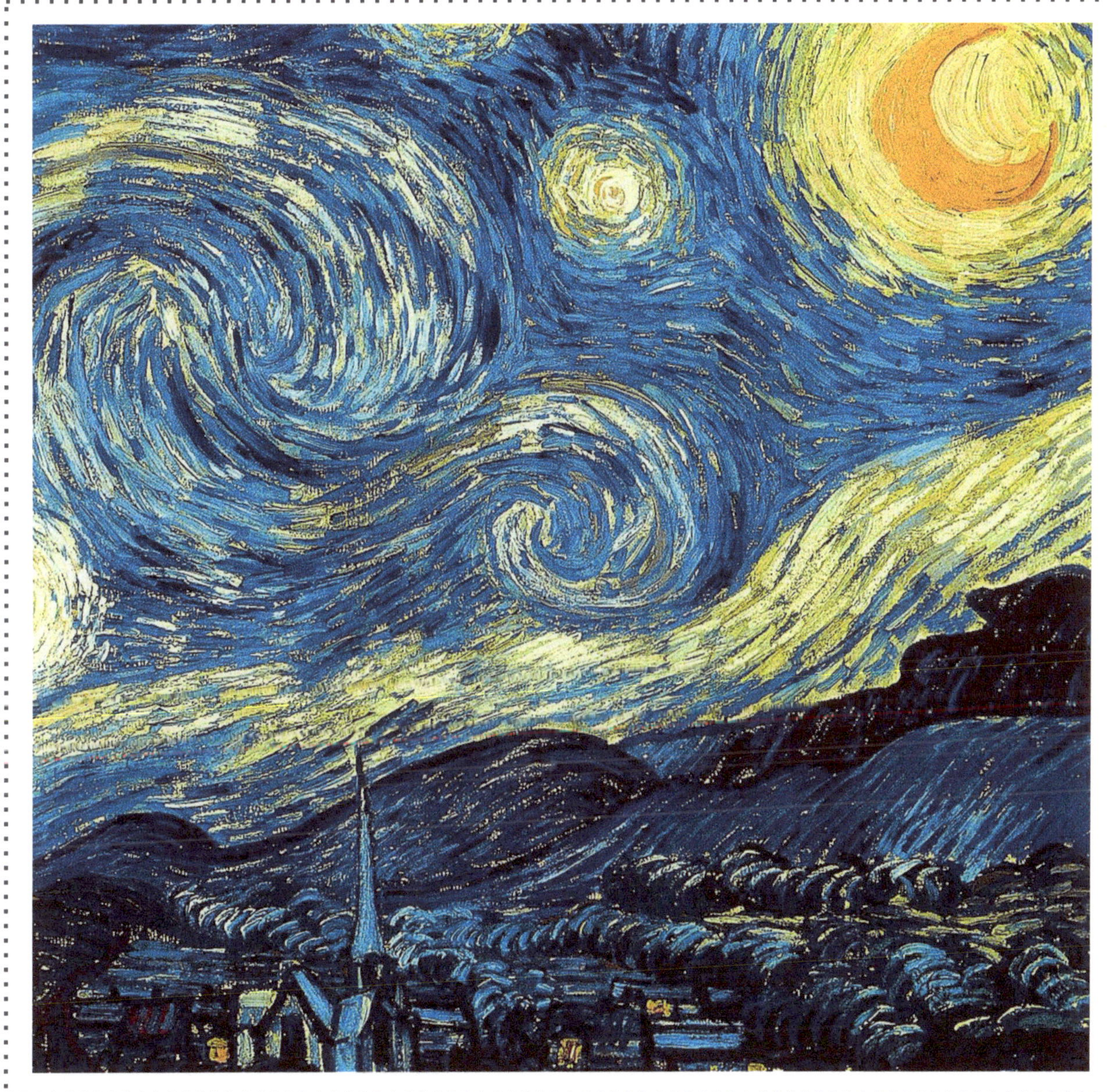

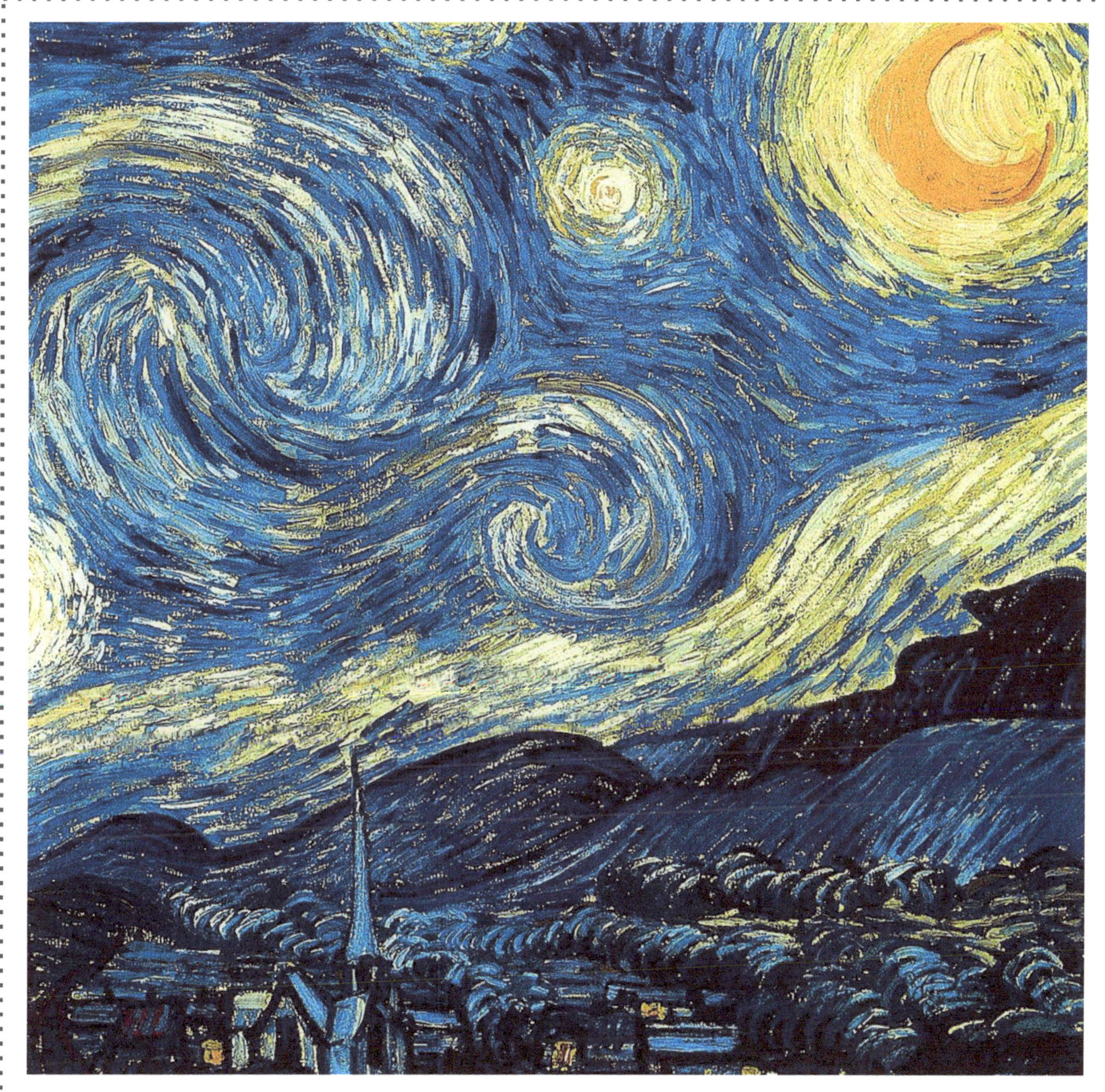

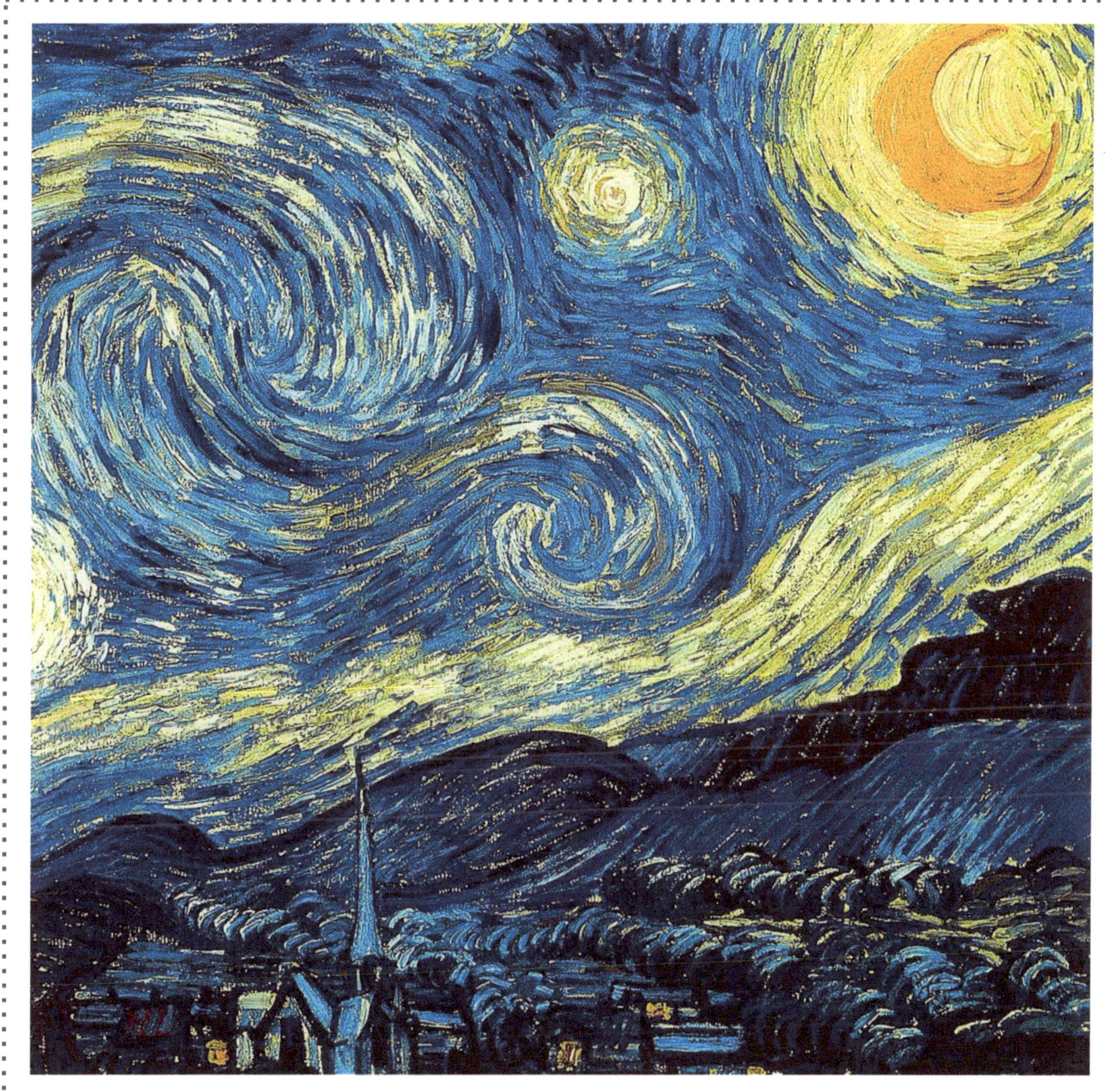

To remove cut along the dotted line.

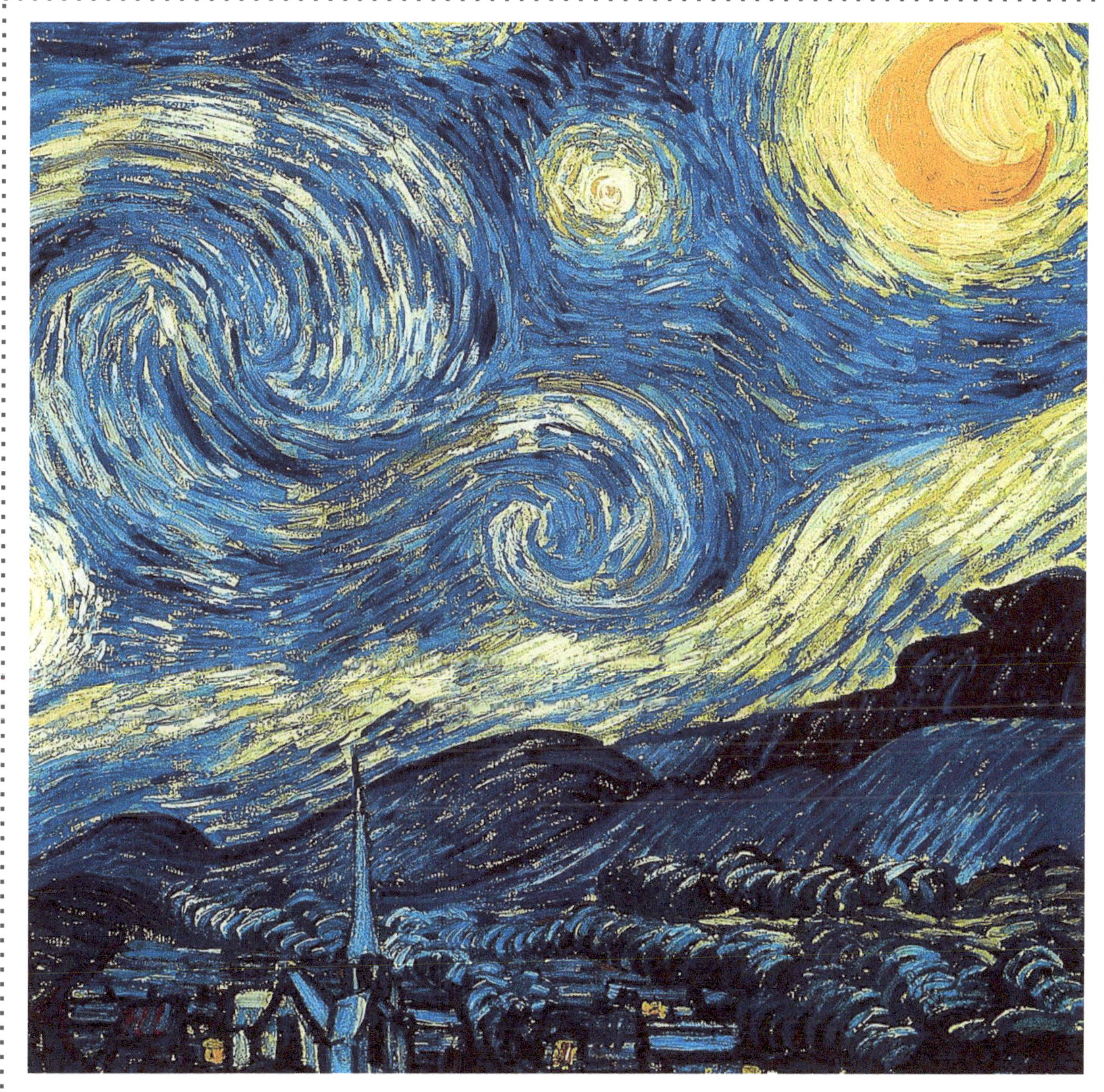

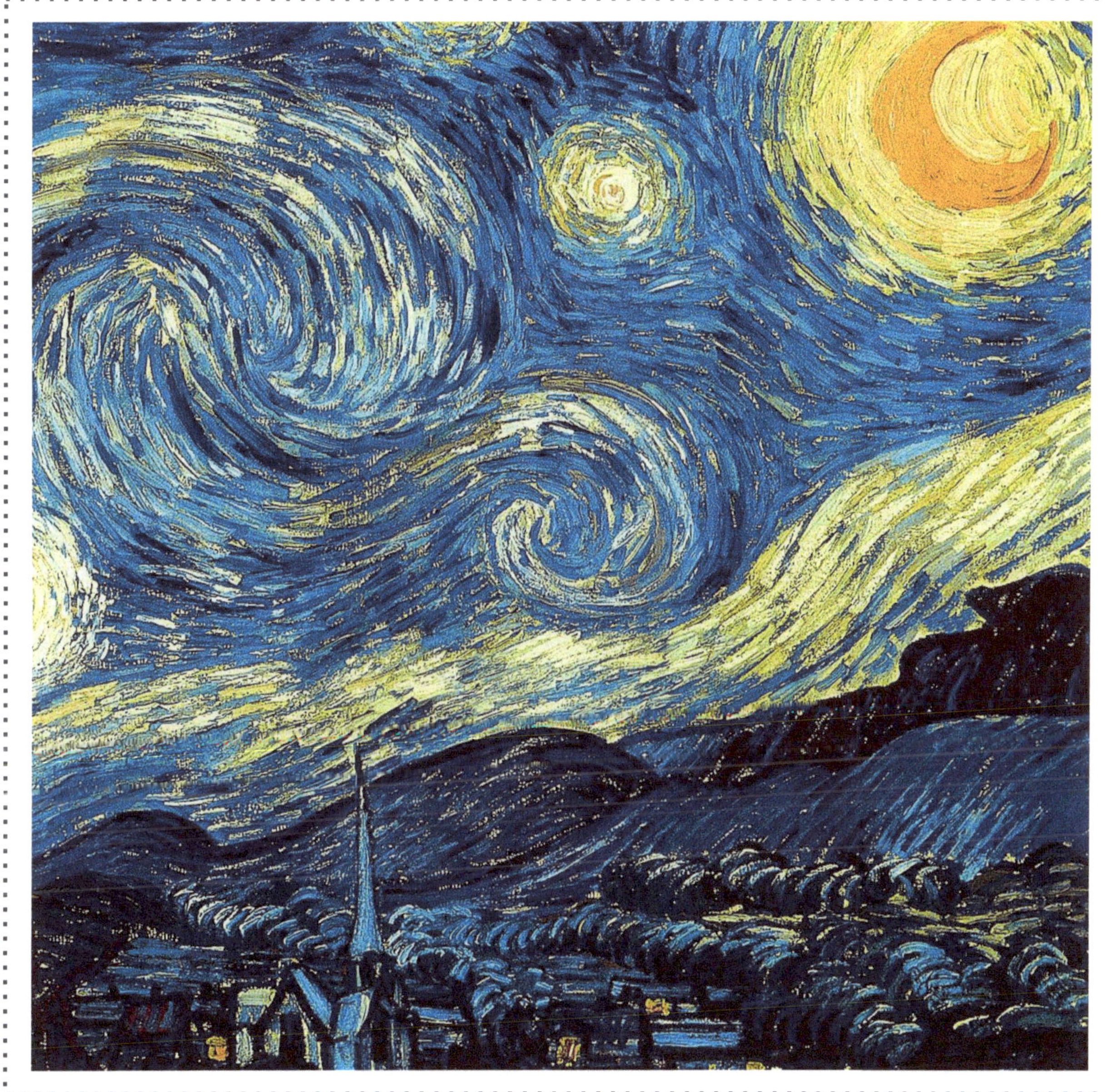

9 781636 572109